Arrangements in th

Mervyn Linford

THE HIGH WINDOW

First published in the UK in 2023 by The High Window Press
3 Grovely Close
Peatmoor
Swindon
SN5 5DN
Email: abbeygatebooks@yahoo.co.uk

Mervyn Linford 2023
ISBN 978-1-913201-90-6

Designed and typeset in Palatino Linotype
by The High Window Press.

Cover photograph and design © Clare Harvey

By the Same Author

Poetry

Two Essex Poets
(with Frederic Vanson)
Talking to the Bees
Collected Poems
Credo
The Saxon Shore
Meanderings
The Killing of the Crystal Tigers
Imagined Essex
Shepherd's Warning

Country Journals

Journey down the Stour
Reflections
Dengie Diaries
Coggeshall Chronicles
Notes from the Fields
The Incidental Marshman

Autobiography

The Willow Pond
Bullshit & Bootlace Ties
The Incomplete Dangler
The Angler's Other Eye

The drunkenness of things being various

(From the poem Snow by Louis MacNeice)

CONTENTS

Apologia for writing nature poetry   9

Summer   14

Off Pat   15
Summer Tench Remembered   16
Silver Coins   17
Bees at an Angle   18
Creed   19
Summer Solstice   20
Weatherwise in June   22
Balsam & Bijouterie   23
August the First   24
Cleg o'clock beside the River   26
What Inspires Transpires   27
Hawthorn Thicket   28
Aliens   30
A Greengage for a Kiss   31
Fleets & Marshes   32
The Legume and the Rose   34
I'm a lover of ring doves   35

Autumn   36

Towards Autumn   37
Geraniums in September   38
The Leaves of Time   39
Three Particles in Blue Air   40
Susurrus in November   41
Beaufort Speaks and the Rain Replies   42
Seven Swans Times Two   43
Tall Trees & Virginia Creeper   44
Easter on the Edge of Advent   45

'Light Verse'   46
Clueless   47
Hard Graft but Worth the Effort   48
A Letter to a Loved One   49
Snared by the Angled Light   50
Wind (for Louis MacNeice)   52
How many Pecks make a Purpose   53
Time in a Timeless Moment   54
Two Tree or not Two Tree*   55
Arrangements in the Key of Light   56
A Rose in October   58
Fall Back – Spring Forward   60

Miscellaneous   61

Plants & Purposes   62
Robin's Pincushion   63
Sparrowhawk in the Rain   64
Camp   66
Horizons & Events   68
A Word about the Logos   69
Songs of Light   70
Unenclosed   71
The Ash Tree and the Moon   72
Phishing   73
The Inspectorate of Spectres   74
Panning the mind for Rudd   76
Glances and Glissando*   77
Heavy Metal – A Requiem   78
Poppies in June (for Sylvia Plath)   79
Echium   80
Echium (2)   81
Denouement   82
Principles and Possibilities   83
Lines   84

Minnows	85
"Words" (for Edward Thomas)	86
Storm Ellen 18th August 2020	87
It's not all Black and White	88
Winter	89
Oilseed Rape – A Carol	90
Something to Wish Upon	91
Frost – New Year's Day	92
Lavenham Woods in Winter	93
Two of a Kind	94
Out of Obscurity	95
Crystal Saints	96
Angels – Gaudete Sunday	98
Wintry	99
Sea Reach & Sandbanks	100
Between the Trees at Midnight	101
Winter Solstice – A Dilemma	102
A Moment in the Mist	104
The Drumbeat of the Stars	105
Snow at Midnight	106
A Fox at Dawn	108
Spring	110
Weathering	111
Two Rooks –Two Species	112
Crime Report	113
Stall Light	114
Art Lesson	115
Waiting for a Bite	116
An Exhumation of the Mind	117
August in May	118
Ai Ai*	119

One Thought – Infinite Expressions 120
True Love 121
A Concrete Proposal 122
Angel 124
Hedge Sparrow (for W H Davies) 125
An Unwritten Stanza 126
Starstruck without Theories without Strings 128
The Borderlands of Light 129
Fingerpost - February 130

Apologia for
Writing Nature Poetry

I've been writing and publishing poetry and prose for nearly fifty years. Most of my work concerns itself with the natural environment – though not exclusively. I do occasionally write poems and prose on other subjects including: politics, satire and human relationships. Over the years I have submitted poems to many magazines, newspapers and periodicals. I have had my share of success and have been published in a number of well know and well respected literary outlets. I have also had more than my fair share of rejections – which is normal for a writer and only to be expected.

What saddens me is the response I've had from some – though not all, by any means – poetry editors. Rejections I can cope with, it's par for the course, but rudeness I can do without. One particular editor – no names no pack drill – ended his rejection slip in reference to my nature poems by writing: "you obviously have some descriptive talent but why don't you write about something with some blood in it." "Nature red in tooth and claw", I presume!

Constructive criticism is both valuable and much appreciated but crass, not to say patronising, inane and unnecessary comments, are something I and no doubt the rest of us can do without. Are the likes of Edward Thomas, Norman MacCaig, Seamus Heaney, Ted Hughes, Frances Cornford or Emily Dickinson to be castigated for writing nature poetry? Not to mention the legions of contemporary poets who concern themselves with nature and the environment. I think not. In fact I think it was Edward Thomas who said something along the lines of: "all poetry is in essence nature poetry".

What did he mean by this remark? For me personally it means that everything we see around us has been created by chemical processes in the heart of the stars in our mysterious and magnificent universe; everything – even the lines upon this page. And if that's not nature in action, then I don't know what is. My poetry in general concerns itself with the cycles of our lives, the cycles of the seasons, and their correspondences. Politics, satire, human relationships and much else besides are important and worth writing about, of course they are, but none of these things or aspects of temporal reality would exist without nature. They are, as I've intimated, the earthly manifestations of stardust.

I spent many years trying in my own mind to resolve the socio, political, environmental and economic realities of the world we inhabit. To think any of us can resolve the world's ills in totality is hubris in the extreme and in my case the mental effort involved resulted in two nervous breakdowns, time spent in psychiatric hospital, and many years of depression. For all my attempts at trying to understand the reality of the world as I experience it, and to find some sort of resolution in my own mind to the socio/economic factors behind human existence it seems that the world is in many ways just as bad now, if not worse, than it was when I was politically radical and engaged in earnest and fully supportive of a vast number of different political, environmental and spiritually orientated groups and organisations.

For me the poetry of nature is not an escape from our existential reality, nor is it simply a consolation to fall back on in the face of a modern, war torn, urban and industrialised consumer orientated society. It is for me personally a *raison d'etre*. To write about the noble, spiritual and creative side of humanity is for my part an attempt in my own small way to counterbalance the ignoble, materialistic and destructive side of our man made and man perpetuated insanities. Nature poetry, I suggest, is nothing other than expression of who we are, where we've come from, and ultimately in what direction we're heading. It is in fact a gauge by which our lives and our connections to the planet we live on are judged, and, in my humble opinion, not an irrelevance but a genuine and necessary creative endeavour. Personally, I don't in general write what I think I should write but I write what I have to write – that which in effect writes me.

In the last fifty years the world's population has doubled and at the same time the species of flora and fauna on our planet have been halved. I suppose like many nature poets I could write propaganda pieces but does poetry 'boil an egg' as Auden once queried? On every level there are more than enough people looking at the rest of us down the end of a long wagging finger. I never really found protest poetry to my liking. I may well agree with much of what the eco poets say but I am still not sure that the way they say it will make any difference in the long run, no more that it has with all the political poetry I remember from the Sixties. I still want to write about nature because I respond and always have responded to wildlife, the weather, landscapes and seascapes with a physical and psychological immediacy that has never really left me since childhood. It's not just an obsession but more of an absolute need to express the seemingly inexpressible. I need to record my awestruck perceptions of these existential mysteries but sadly only have the clumsy and less than adequate tool of language to work with. I am not talking about some sort of pastoral escapism or the belief in the often mythologised Golden Age. I am also fully aware of the hardships involved when working on the land as I have done so myself from time to time. I also know that 'all things bright and beautiful' has its opposite i.e. 'all things dark and ugly'. The age of the hunter/gatherer has gone and is not likely to return unless the lights go out or we succumb to nuclear war. I'm just trying in a more celebratory and transformative way to highlight what we've lost and what we're losing. For all the problems environmentally, politically, socially, I still have a deep and indelible sense of the oneness of reality.

Most of my draught work is written outdoors and I often feel that it is nature that is writing me instead of the other way round. Whatever we and our hubris do to Mother Earth that oneness will still exist with or without us. As a number of physicists are beginning to say – the universe seems more like a great thought than anything else. The dazzling darkness, the thoughtless all-knowing 'thinks' and then material reality is manifested in all its multifaceted forms. Just like String Theory where the different vibrations determine the different elements. Imagine an ocean where on the surface all of the waves are differentiated but underneath all is one. My poetry has more to do with quantum physics and the ancient mystery religions than it has to do with putting the world to rights. If it achieves anything tangibly effective as far as the environmental degradation we are experiencing nowadays is concerned then that is a welcome by-product. I write mainly as a way of questioning how we are formed by and relate to the wider environment through language which in a way is the very mechanism that puts a barrier between us and that all-encompassing sense of indivisibility. I use highly wrought, figurative and associative language to move away from mere description in the vain hope that I might at least occasionally connect more fully with the *genius loci* at a slant as opposed to head-on.

SUMMER

Off-Pat

If I were a buttercup
which I'm not
or might
be

I'd shine a light on you beneath your chin
like the light that shone when children were alive
     to each new sensation.

Not as now when I name the flower 'little frog'*
or prefix its golden glory with such sins as:
meadow, creeping, bulbous or the things
     of old Linnaeus –

there'd be no Latin language like the mass:
that far forgotten mystery occluded by furtive priests –

there'd be just you and me and this small bloom
to prove that hearts still churn and love still matters
when buds expand and blossom in the heat
     and the bee advances.

*Ranunculus is the Latin name for the buttercup and it means 'little frog' –probably because many species of the plant flower close to or even in the water.

Summer Tench Remembered

Those early mornings in late June
when we cycled down the dog rose scented lanes
      towards the lake

are still a far remembrance I can touch
as tangible as this slow moving pen
between my ageing fingers and a thumb
      and reminiscence.

When pipistrelles and swallows changing place
across the face of still reflective water
enhanced the baited moment and our faith
      in the feeding tench.

Between the lily's chalices of gold
upheld to catch the honeyed light of dawn
a thousand pin-prick bubbles effervesced like our resolve
      and corked anticipation.

I'm there right now in images and icons
reflected and refracted through the mind
like time dissolved in light's unfathomed depths

as a slippery olive dream with sunset eyes
thrashes at the surface of a lake
and I in the factual absence of a net
      scoop up the prize.

Silver Coins

Summer has flipped a coin and the reverse is autumn:
not yet July but the rain has truly tarnished what was mint
     in the month of May.

There are no flames, no fire, only the veils of drizzle to explain
the sodden landscape. Silver is the birch tree and the clouds
when time like a niggard Midas
pockets a golden sovereign in his shrouds
     for the fear of spending.

And now to add the last inclement insult
the gods of summer's dark and chill arcades
    have pulled the silver handle

        - tic - tac - toe -

                    and down the chute
              comes all of light's

lost change

in a drench

of shillings.

Bees at an Angle

In our front garden we have the leaning tower of echium
        – or is it Babel?

The language is that of pollen and of nectaries
as the bees of many different buzzing kinds
climb this green and lilac conic plant
with its slanted flowers
towards the sun.

Honey is the reason and the rhyme for these congregations -
these biblical brown words in velveteen
and the plushest verses.

And what is the denouement of each chapter
as the metaphor drips sweetness from each cell
and light between each synapse is translated
to a wordless universal non-idea
        without a sting?

Creed

As the wind dies back the summer returns:
swifts, no longer out of place, screech around
the eaves in black formations – in bursts
of explosive sound. The sky is cloudless:
a blue unbounded silence unrehearsed
as the earth in slow succession counters

death with a loud performance. What's been lifted
are the weather's shrouds. Ascendance rises
with the lark – the thermals. We have the sun's
soliloquy of light, its many gifts:
the stridulation of ideas, the timeless-
ness of now, the doves' syllabics – wonder.

Summer Solstice

It's warming up and June and the flaming saw
      have come together:

the weather and the cliché will be one
      when the god arises.

The sun is at its stationary zenith
      – its solstice –

for three whole days its heat and its position
      will remain in a solar stasis
          and round the stones the druids
             will succumb to pagan thoughts

   and the
thoughtless summer.

Their golden age is hung in the blue infinity of light
like a ducat or doubloon that's never spent –
that knows no profit.

Their coffers are a cache of ancient rites
where all they gather glisters and belongs –
is offered up, a solstice sacrifice,
like a butchered
auroch.

And on the 303 the traffic drones
as it makes its way from London to the coast
where Kernow waits with wishing wells and pixies
and old Pendragon's son, that bright Arcturus,
is hung like another symbol in the sky
      as Monmouth simmers.

Three days and the summer liturgy complies
        with a Christian doctrine –

the three in one of December's light incarnate
and the text of stones and tombs
and the thorn that flowers

at a time when the Nordic fire burns with ice
or adds to the words and wishes and the gifts
that Sleipnir and the patriarch of Christmas

give with the bold largesse of a golden tongue –
a lexicon that's written by the scribes
of history's acknowledged myths and magi
        as the sun arises.

Weatherwise in June

It's always the weather that inspires:
why this should be does not escape my senses
as the blue of this June day intensifies
and the leaves on the tallest lime
hang listless in the gilded morning air
     and the doves' recitals.

I lie here in the grass like any snake
whose midnight blood needs sunlight's warm transfusion
     and a mind that's still.

I can hear and it's not tinnitus or the music
that the ancients thought a product of the spheres:
the thermocline between the earth and heavens

that separates our breath from the breathless stars –
a whisper like the sea, a susurration in the oceanic backdrop
   of a prayer without religion.

And rare yet commonplace, like a mute idea,
the blackbird is a quest and not a question
as it opens wide the trope of its golden bill
to flare with song as the photons spill and fledge
     from a nest unanswered.

Balsam & Bijouterie

Year on year the temperatures increase
and this afternoon in August claims a record.*

It is cloudless and the air is blue with heat
    – like a contradiction –

geraniums are red as are the stems of the flowering balsam
more appropriate as metaphors to speak in the name of fire.

The sun at the blinding zenith of the sky
        – enflames –

      but not with passion
           but conceits that
                are more lethargic.

           The fashion for accessories this summer
       like the rose of Sharon's gold bijouterie
will be the mounts for jewel-like honeybees
       and the light in amber.

*40.3C was recorded at Coningsby in Lincolnshire on 19 July 2022.

August the First

First Fruits and the harvest of the wheat have come together:
Loafmas appropriately, as the heat and the dust of August
    fill the air with the sense of endings.

Toadflax and willowherb
        speak of something other than a feast
                as the headlands start to dry
                        and slowly wither.

This is the weather made for swifts and spiders
for glittering geometries of light
that radiate the diamond cut of dawn
or mention without words those dark migrations
        beneath the stars.

Lammas, another word for plums and damsons –
for summer's sweet fruition on the tongue
      and the tainted lips

when the bloom upon the purples of their skin
is as misted as September's fated kiss
      and the thoughts of frost.

All in the garnered moment:
   loss and plenty, the falling sap –
      apples in the store, ash and embers
         glowing in the grate as the shadows lengthen.

The barn is stacked with straw up to its eaves
and like the bow that's drawn across the strings
      of the mournful cello

                              the yellowing of leaves
                    and gathered swallows
              ease into something
summer has composed
in a minor
  key.

All that juice and all that joy is now the grist
that autumn's mill must grind into dust or powder
like the scales on the wings of butterflies when touched
            by the hands of time.

Cleg o'clock beside the River

It starts again – the deluge:
no antediluvian sense of the perfect summer
can reign as does the rain that now descends
    in silver wires.

I cannot part these verticals that scan
from thunder clouds to the parched and drinking earth
  with their molten metals.

At best, like birds hunched-up beneath the leaves,
I'll sit within the shelter and the din of this green umbrella

and as the river's strafed by shards and shrapnel
and the sky is riven wide by the snaking light

I'll watch the frightened cattle hoist their tails
and run from the clegs' advances through the willows
into the open meadow and the veils
    of abysmal weather.

What Inspires Transpires

Different leaves make different sounds:
the alder whispers, the willow sighs,
	the poplar rattles.

These are the summer words that should inspire
but the heat is such that lethargy conceives
	of only silence.

I am dumb to speak the purposes of song
when the ring doves drop hot syllables of lead
	and the rhythm falters.

What is mute, devoid of meaning, without voice
is poised to raise an altar to the sun
	as thought transpires

and as the photons fathom one by one,
like phonemes in the larynx
		of this verse

stomata like a sacrament reserved
transform or transubstantiate the light
	without a word.

Hawthorn Thicket

It was dark then in the thicket
when summer's leaves hardly spoke
and the slant of the sun was quick
between the silence. The elm rose

into the blue and I too foot
by careful foot climbed to a height
above the shades below and looked
towards the marsh. Not so much sight

as vision when the light and creeks
were one in a silver dazzle.
I have been back, often – this week
in fact. Was it the same? The dash

and shatter of the tide still shone
but didn't sparkle. The tall elm
has shrunk to nothing. My shins
and knees intact, not scuffed, the self

overactive perhaps – not quite
overwhelmed. I must be truthful:
the thicket's gone, the elm tree writes
its own sick epitaph, and beauty

is atavistic – memory.
There is still the darkness of course,
the silence, diagonal seams
of light, motes – gold dust. I can walk

to the creeks and marshes, they still
exist, have escaped the planner,
the bricks – concrete. Even the hill
that stood between me and the land

I thought I ruled has lost its church
and all sense of meaning. Can time
remove it all? Those early verses
without words – the unknown sublime?

Today, somewhere else, diagonal
shafts of light through surviving elms –
wych elms perhaps. There is magic
admittedly, a silent realm

that whispers, stirs something. The past?
I'm not sure. Nature's voice? Maybe.
At the other end of starlight
when night is close to the day –

when there's more hope than certitude
and the end more like a beginning
the whisper is its loudest. Blue
between the leaves, boundless, singing.

All thickets are the same it seems,
time and place lost, non-existent.
What dapples is not light, not dreams –
the leaves are speaking. Stop. Listen.

Aliens

Tangled or tousled, not hair
but a swamp and copse
    beside the river.

Hemp agrimony, dropwort and the air
misted and enlightened by the dawn
accept the sunlit angles, slanted, rare,
that splay between the ash trees
and the willows and a mass of ivy.

It's almost somewhere else
   – one expects lianas –
                                 exotic birds
                    or primates
             hanging fruits.

But this is the Suffolk border into Essex
where the alien is a swathe of purple balsam
and I who have lived immersed in this river's glare
  am right now a migrant.

A Greengage for a Kiss (*Compulsory Purchase* 1950s*)

Why should a greengage
taste like a summer's day
       in the 1950s?

What succulence, seductive as it was,
when love, first love, perhaps infatuation,
tainted the teeth and tongue and these young lips
    with forbidden fruit?

That time in a certain garden close to home
where the steam trains rattled past on their way to London
and that shack with its boarded windows and a well
a reminder of such lives that were there undone
    by a dream of housing.

And where do I dwell right now
after the post-war years and the rationed love

       of that cold estate –

now that lust and the greengage days of another life
have aged into something golden like the leaves
    that are frail and fallen?

The veins in the flesh of light is where I live
estranged from the summer's heat and that wild garden
and although my heart resists the kiss of time
       and its dark rebuffal
the night and the frigid moon and the loveless stars
       find me unrequited.

**The plotland shacks and houses that were demolished
       to make way for Basildon New Town*

Fleets & Marshes

The swans' eggs were our quest –
the holy grail of innocence that met
at the meeting place of sunrise and the fleets
    – the holy voices –

the plainsong of the curlew and the geese –
the liturgy and littorals of light
where oystercatchers, chasuble and surplus,
bleeped along the reaches and the curves
        of the tidal waters.

I hear some Roman words and taste the salt
as oyster shells and medieval pilgrims
survey the eastern precincts of the sky
and pray for peace - or else redemption.

The ooze between the toes, the glaucous prospect,
where purslane and sea lavender repose
amongst the shrubby seablite and the swathes
of scurvy grass and sea pinks and the zones
of bleaching exoskeletons and claws that will not close –

        that will not open.

Beyond the fleets, the dykes, the blown phragmites,
the haunts of bearded reedlings and the coots –
towards the coast of Hoo and Grain and Sheppey
where the sunstruck shores of Kent and the Thames on fire
        were a burning question:

the after dawn confession on our knees
before the reeds and rushes of a shrine; a desecration –

was neither a transgression or redeemed
by the oystercatcher's image of a priest
     or the sky's blue ovum.

The Legume and the Rose

Everlasting pea and iceberg roses
legumes and thoughts of love
as the summer ends
and the sun

forecloses.

It's nearly dusk and the fragrance is not strong
      – not the scent of musk –

as the season thinks of moths
            and the midnight hush
                  of the moon's enticements.

Nitrogen is fixed as are the stars
but the planets wander on around the arc
      of a cold ecliptic.

There is no chart, no course that I can plot
only the things and theories that we know

      – the ones we love –

the elements, the cycles and that sense, a subtle feeling
that the iceberg though anaemic fills with blood
and the everlasting legume builds our bones
   and the light's aorta.

I'm a lover of ring doves

but to others they are nothing more than pigeons
            – wood pigeons –

Farmers hate them:
shotguns, gas guns, air guns, anything
to cull their numbers is the *modus operandi.*

For me their silver greys, suffusing pinks
and the white yet broken ring that speaks their name
            is my betrothal.

There's a certain iridescence
      – a rainbow sheen –
that marks them out as treasure
with no X to mark the spot.

They are for me a feathered crock of gold that isn't metal
and when I see them rise and clap their wings
to applaud it seems their own resplendent selves
I know that air upholds such splendid things
without a prayer or profit –
      even purpose.

AUTUMN

Towards Autumn

There is a haze of purple, maybe mauve,
where the mallow grows along the summer verge
and the skylark high on something, maybe song,
        is a singing star.

A black star, punctuation, but no full stop
as the notes that may be mauve or may be purple
drop from a sky that's glacial and blue
with cumuli and golden intimations
as the clouds in caravanserai pass through
        on their way to autumn.

Geraniums in September

Even in September the geraniums
are hot and red and fiery.

They have passion
as the grey autumnal mist
chills the pallid flesh down to the bones.

Their tone is harsh and loud
as the aftermath of summer and the harvest
sinks like the setting sun into winter's shrouds
    and the frosted stars.

Hot and red and fiery like my love
when the spring was vibrant.

But now the glowing embers
in the grate of a soft September.

And like the falling leaves and the fallen sap
now that my burning heart is an autumn pyre

    – a landlocked ghat –

defined by the smoke and ash of all that's left
of my love and the word desire and these flowers
    as they gash and smoulder.

The Leaves of Time

It's time to kick and shuffle through the leaves:
to wear the boots we wore when we were young –
when we believed that autumn was enough
    and that fun was endless.

To find the roots of laughter as the leaves
exploded into air from summer's embers –
when grief was counteracted by each leaf,
the golden light, expansive and asunder,
and all we knew of winter and despair
was the joy of snow, the whiteness and the wonder
      of being born.

Three Particles in Blue Air

Two crows in the clear blue air of St Luke's October
configure what's disputed in the glare
with a sparrowhawk that circles as it dares
    to ignore their protest.

And then the three protagonists are one
in some explicit form made up of orbits.

The sparrowhawk the nucleus aware
of the proton and electron as they flare
    around the centre.

This subatomic metaphor may stretch
the bounds of possibility, that's true,
but then the quantum principle's uncertain
as what I see is altered by my sight.

So what I write is either true or false
as crows and one lone sparrowhawk disport
in strange antagonistic airy circles
where blue and even gold are far less fraught
    than a verse unfathomed.

Susurrus in November

If you listen to the silence
November brings to misted fields and rivers
when the song-less skies traversed by pure white swans
are cold ideas of frost and winter snow
and the robin in the thicket by the weir
looks to the blue yet blear remembered light
    in its red resplendence

you will hear the cattle graze beside the willows –
a whisper that was summer in the air
when leaves were hung in vibrant strings of green
before the world was yellowing and old
    and the trees denuded

and yet right here, right now, the robin's song
appears from the mist and silence, chill and thin,
where the water combs its venerable hair
across the sill and susurrus that spins
into the weir pool's quick revolving wheels
    that are sheer yet soundless.

Beaufort Speaks and the Rain Replies

After a night of rain and storm force winds
the meadow beside the river is a scene of devastation:

branches and boughs and leaves are strewn abroad
where the spate that rushes by and bends the reeds
is a debris-ridden viscous muddy hoard
        of a summer's ruins.

What floods is what floods the mind
        when October darkens:

when the gates and sluices open to the skies
and the truth of St Luke's
calm weather

is a lie
            as the wind
                        increases.

Across the grey inclemency of cloud
a heron lumbers heavenwards on wings
        made of nimbostratus

as the rain once more relentless in its shrouds
obscures the light and limits all but vision
except where the leaves in gold chaotic showers
direct the eyes to a plumage in eclipse
        like the wreck of angels.

Seven Swans Times Two

Seven swans upending in the river
holding themselves against the raging current
        as they try to feed.

Seven swans above the gleaming gold
    of the rounded pebbles

as a buzzard soars and circles and submerges
    like a drowning icon.

This is September green amongst the hills
that curve and climb or fall to their own reflections
between the unbounded verticals of trees
        as they delve and double.

Seven swans and the drift of yellow leaves
that flood and fathom earthwards in the air
or tessellate the surface and the willows
that sound the soundless river and a mist
        as it preens and purples.

Seven swans that stretch their meanings and their necks
as their webbed assault in unison achieves
a heavenwards ascension into blue
and a white descendent mute
subconscious theme
of the light
divided.

Tall Trees & Virginia Creeper

There is no movement in the leaves –
save for sporadic speechless slow detachments
in gold and scarlet.

The weather speaks in misty greys and purple –
a lonely dark soliloquy of light with no reply.

Answers are what they are in dark October
when like a grief in weeds of mourning colour
the summer's widow bleeds from a broken heart
as the creeper reddens.

What's spoken now is silence thus translated
into the muted music and the themes of a final poem
where the sift and susurration of the air

with gold and scarlet whispers
in their reams on the written grass
are the winter's cold preamble and its dream

of an icy coda.

Easter on the Edge of Advent

Wherever I am there's a robin:
this morning beside the river and a gate
that is galvanised and grey on the edge of silver
this small red-breasted totem or familiar
out of the river's spate like a sudden undine
makes its rare yet somehow commonplace appearance
    like a muse or magus.

This epiphany, this Advent out of air strange visitation
could be a giant star or the voice of Mars
or anything on the bar of a metal gate
as it opens onto pasture and a river
that floods the mind with thoughts and weird relations
    and a splash of blood.

'Light Verse'

Berries or blood what's the difference?
These corpuscles of hips and autumn haws
coagulate in hedgerows as the leaves
    begin to tarnish.

These blisterings that feed the hungry birds
and prime the living pulse in winter's veins
become the fieldfare's heart
    the blackbird's song

and sow the seeds that propagate the summer
with arteries and oxygen, stomata
that breathe the greening chemistry of light
    and fill my lungs.

Clueless

Down the air the first of autumn's leaves
incline towards October and a breath
    that barely whispers.

There is a slant, a drift of tarnished words,
that say in a thousand mute soliloquies
    what's been said before.

This reprise we know of old,
when our gold becomes pyrites and the song
belongs to the silken treble, the lament,
that the robin weaves like fate
    or the webs of spiders.

We are snared by the thoughts of time and a lost belief
as frost and a sense of winter and despair
are caught like a leaf that trembles as it hangs
from the tangled threads that are clueless; every strand –
    taut – yet tenseless.

Hard Graft but Worth the Effort

Who needs a red, red, rose when mine are yellow?
Is love by any other name so different?
When the swallows come and the swifts
       that always follow

fly around my eaves and this small garden
will the fragrance and the heat of any summer
be any more or less because of yellow instead of red?

And love as you and I have always known
will always bud and flower in the spring
and even now as autumn shows its colours

with faded leaves as petals shed and scatter
this yellow rose, not jaundiced, not fool's gold,
is all to me that matters like two hearts
       that time has grafted.

A Letter to a Loved One

There are irises between the yellow roses –
they too are yellow but in a way more jaundiced
and their blooms are striped with brown.

Does this distract from beauty
    – you tell me –

so many things are tainted, somehow tarnished,
but even rust and verdigris have charms
  as they say in France

je ne sais quoi.

Old age it's said adds value to antiques:
a certain something –
a patina

and as the leaves in autumn and my veins
become not symbiotic but analogous

I hope when turning life's unwritten page
the fox marks and the rages and my sins
    will still excite you.

Snared by the Angled Light

There is an image that is fixed, that never leaves me:
an orchard in the Plotlands close to autumn
where sunlight at an angle through the trees
      is splayed and shafted.

The darkness of that orchard is relieved
by golden pears - so hung – like Chinese lanterns
and plums so ripe and rounded, ruby red,
that I can taste the succulence right now
      on this dry tongue.

The back-path is the place, the early centre,
that still succumbs to my chaotic mind
    when in need of grounding:

The motes, those points of light beyond the privet –
the shining ones that shimmered when my sight
      was full of angels

are still
      I know
           not where
                inside or out
                    a sacred vision.

The silence without birdsong and the light
that sparkled on the diadem's soft snares
is still a rare unspoken mute idea
that radiates September
and the years
as time

ferments.

The scent that brings a greengage to the lips
or the bloom that turns the damson into mist
    and thoughts of frost
is never lost when the centre reappears
      like a living ghost.

Wind *(for Louis MacNeice)*

Let it be said that the weather is various –
that the wind with its western edges
hones more than ploughshares and the dykes
  that are swords and sabres.

Here where the harrier quarters over reeds
and the tractor trawls the season to its end
    with a catch of gulls.

Let it be said that thistledown is tantamount to snow
as it drifts at a tangent to the times
and the climate is the drunkenness of dusk
  and the toadflax – candles.

Here where the North Sea glows and the land is lambent –
where between the lens and the light and a million starlings
there is more than one supposes or assumes
as the moon through its breathless phases still intones
    an intoxication.

How many Pecks make a Purpose?

They peck at nothing
    or so it seems
the ring doves on my lawn.

They peck beneath geraniums and roses –
the red and yellow products and the schemes
    of my green fingers.

I ask them why and in a way they answer
with their slow syllabic summer haunted themes
    of heat and thermals.

They peck at variations
    – leitmotivs –

of bees and random helices of white
as butterflies convolve and dust in spirals
rises and repeats the air's advice
    across the fields.

A strange enigma this in shades of pink –
the yellow eye, the bill, the blue
    – besilvered –

that makes me think that nothing must exist
as toadflax touches autumn
and the mist

                 is snared by
            silken moments
      and the gist
of something
  other.

Time in a Timeless Moment

Time is in the tone of every leaf:
each red and yellow clock –
each fallen second

that cloaks the earth with sentiments like grief
and leaves the trees to winter and their bones
    as they crack and whiten.

The oak and ash have metaphors not answers
as smoke from autumn fires - time's reprise,
climbs into blear and hazy blue September
    that fashions out of air
        obscurities

    like mist and
        meanings.

The spring that isn't spring is winding down
and down the daylit thermocline
        belief
        is also falling.

The red and yellow moments – leitmotivs,
describe what is invisible
yet seen

as space and this strange jigsaw made of leaves
is framed for a frozen instant and redeemed
    by the missing piece.

Two Tree or not Two Tree*

My favourite place has almost disappeared –
not from the face of earth you understand
but under the grey October veils of rain
    as the seascape brightens.

Like fog with the sun behind it light responds
    with a rare candescence

and the tide between the asters and the ooze
holds up its level glass to the hidden sky
    and the geese reflected.

All is a blanching prize to the careful eye
that chances on the dunlin and the knot
who fly in flocks like smoke from autumn fires
    as they swirl and whisper.

And as the rain releases these far vistas
that I have known through every changing season
another murmuration gilds the sight
as sun-shafts splay and slant across the creeks
    and the clear horizon.

Starlings spiral down the sky's blue stair
into the trees ignited by the spark of a warm idea
before the stars at midnight hold the dark in their silver grip
and thoughts become as black as returning geese
    in their skeins unspooling.

*Two Tree Island lies between Leigh-on-Sea and Canvey Island
on the edge of the Thames Estuary*

Arrangements in the Key of Light

When the weather changes so do I:
three days of rain and cloud
more like a mist

that clips the tops of trees and shrouds the hills
leaves me in a place where the will dissolves
    as the mind deranges.

If there's a rift in this October's greyness
allowing a shaft of sunlight through the gloom
to lift my leaden spirits
rearrange

what we assume as autumn's dying corpus
into the tomb of winter and its bones
    all blanched and brittle

then this place will be far more than hints or phrases
that relate doom-laden messages of time and light's demise

    and so will I.

I will write as the evening text erases blue
and the setting sun in its rook-beleaguered skies
looks to the proof of Venus and a moon
that rises full and round like an amber statement –
a phrase or two that brightens and belies all lunar thoughts
    and the word derangement.

The book will be thus revised by unnumbered stars
and the robin's midnight anthem to the leaves

    as they gently fall

and I and the mist that glitters and the frost
that spreads its pall of whiteness over grass
will accept the cold intentions of the dark
as Orion glances downwards through the night
      on the world's repose

and take as the lonely singer takes his chance
to sing as the axis slopes into a song
that is sung like a note of hope in the silent earth
as the snowdrop grows unseen on a greening stave
      like a new arrangement.

A Rose in October

'By any other name', it's said
   – but I'm not sure –

Now in the mellow month of morning mist and the hint of frost
this yellow rose, this fist from a summer passing
that lingers with its tight determined pose of folded petals
     is a name incarnate.

If I called it something else, a star perhaps,
would it have the same green-fingered bright effect
    on the watching eye?

     – I doubt it –

The evening sky has billions of blooms
that bud and flower nightly with the moon
    but they are not roses.

Is the sun another metaphor for light
when it climbs this October morning into blue
and the misted yellow moment of the rose
unfolds its closed resistance to the dark
   and the thought of winter.

Analogies or truth – what do we know:
a rose, the stars, the sun and our surmisals –
three words that are supposedly three facts
and yet in other languages transposed
     by different letters

these words
are not the thing –
the thought translated.

October slowly mellows into mist
and leaves that capture gold and purple shadows
where a yellow rose unconscious of these facts
exists in its mute unchosen span of time
and I in this lyric language of my own
            detect a kinship.

Fall Back – Spring Forward

Grass that once was green is brown and golden.
The cold and the detachment of the leaves
that tumble down unconscious of the air or grey October
deceive the eye with thoughts of precious metal
     when all is tarnished.

Our backward glance towards remembered light
     and a fruitful summer

reminds us as we say: *fall back, spring forward,*
that time and the turning seasons can't relax
     in the face of aeons.

Truth is a fact that finds us where we are with what we have
and as I watch the leaves that slant and sidle
adding their gold, that some would call pyrites,

to the autumn spread of alchemy and humus
I know that the clock has hands without a heart
and that nature winds its spring with a hidden movement
     or a play on words.

MISCELLANEOUS

Plants & Purposes

Privet and leylandii, suburbia's green walls –
ways and means of social isolation.

Society's enclosure act
by sheep without a shepherd
obscuring what we'd see if we had eyes
that saw beyond the evergreen beliefs that blind our vision.

We have the tools, the implements it seems,
to cut and fell, to prune and open up our private space
where birds with less restrictions sing and feed
and the nettles gather butterflies and dreams
        that sting the mind.

Robin's Pincushion

As pincushions go, this one, red and rusty
in the rain and without its robin
its meaning or its purpose
seems rather pointless –
   as are its pins

   – its absences.

But what is the point –

angels on one end
and beads of blood
   on the other?

The point is I am here and it is there
and we have made a connection.

Whether or not this gall
or whatever you want to call it understands
is beside – yes – you've guessed it – the point.

Sparrowhawk in the Rain

Travelling back but staying where you are
      is called nostalgia

        – but –

is that a fact, or is it more that memory unites
the disparate reality of time
and who we are
is actually
a pact

between succession's meanings
and the sum of our mental weather.
      And does it matter?

Today the rain that rattles and reacts
unconsciously to my apparent thoughts
is unaware of light and what divides us
as I stare through my study window
and the glass that is not transparent.

And yet this now would not be now at all
without my past and my projected future.

A sparrowhawk like Simeon Stylites
perches on the top of this brown pole
     with its looping wires

as if to say there is communication
without the need to lift that loud receiver
    when the phone is ringing.

I'm in a place right here where I was then
when birds' eggs were a childish *raison d'etre*
and sparrowhawks were watched and time immense
    and summers endless.

That bird has flown and now in the pouring rain
this same yet other feathered apparition
in a drenched and dishevelled moment through the glass
outspreads its wings and melds with tomorrow's weather
    and disappears.

Camp

Memory has its silences:
like that muted, dark and damp far hawthorn thicket
where we used to hide from parents and ourselves
in a makeshift camp made of plywood, felt and tin
        by an open fire.

The sponginess of humus underfoot
and that smell that was always autumn, always dank,
was never enough to discourage our pubescence –
the nakedness, the mutual masturbation,
        the ways of illicit pleasure.

Girls there were and those breathless sexual games
        – those explorations –

but gender was a strange uncertain thing
as our summer skin and the shafts of angled light
played on the bronzing moment and our minds
        that were still divided.

The silences were kept, the secrets dark, and I'm sure
when reading this with your quick assumptions
        you will be wrong

but for many undecided, damp with tears,
in the thickets of their filial relations
as autumn stirs the senses and the air
        holds the scent of winter.

The rack of the Roman Church and its inquisitions
that destroyed their holy chances and the hope of a sinless life
still haunts their every footstep and the silence

as the autumn leaves still spongy underfoot
define two distant moments that connect
      to the disconnected.

Horizons & Events

I am looking elsewhere for the light:
dawn and dusk crepuscular and dim
      are not enough:

one with the light advancing like a flower;
a primrose in the apogee of spring
   when the sun has woken –

the other, light returning to the dark,
where the only hints of something more than ice
      are the distant stars.

I am looking for that singular event
where the light thus spent
is held against its need
to find an eye

by
gravity's
insistence.

Elsewhere – that is – within the death of light
where love is at its brightest:

where I am blind to what we knew of time –
   where in the endless silence

      – undivided –

the lack of words though black and there unspoken
are somehow said through sightless signs and symbols
where the mindless and the meaningless combine
    as if flesh transmuted.

A Word about the Logos

When the sun rises over the meadows and the mist
and the dewdrops on the grass and the farmer's gate
sparkle like a cache of hidden treasure
        that the eye uncovers

it is certain that our sight is redefined
by the sound of light's intensity and silence
        and our altered senses.

                    Perception and reality expand
            to such a wide immensity of seeing
that what was once a landscape
            in the mind

with boundaries and borderlines and facts
                    becomes instead a solar re-enactment

of what
        the heart
                and starlight
                        left unsaid
                                when the

        Word

R-E-S-O-U-N-D-E-D

Songs of Light

I cannot help but sing the songs of light:
rhyme or no is not the thing that matters –
what matters is the music that we bring
    to the weight of words.

What lightens is the rhythm of the heart
that pulses through the veins and every star
        and love's aorta.

The arteries and lungs of every song
inspired by the breath of every leaf and every photon
must feel the beat of galaxies that spin
and all the bright and constellated themes
      of spring and winter.

Summer and autumn also have their songs
that lift the lark or sing of the falling leaves
and each in each the corpuscle is cast
like a leitmotiv in an endless composition.

Perpetuum and mobile it seems
is what we are in a vast symphonic concert
and even though our thoughts, all explanation,
can rely on prose to explicate the themes

it is assonance and consonance and feeling
that here translate the atom and its quanta
into a piece that the voice alone repeats
      like a supernova.

Unenclosed

Sometimes I stop the car in the middle of nowhere
    – if nowhere can have a centre that is.

For a full 360 degrees there is nothing but farmland,
    trees and a few haphazard hedgerows.

In a dip, just before a wooded hill and the far horizon
the church of the Holy Trinity makes its medieval statement.

It says, or perhaps intones would be more appropriate,
that the enclosures and the common land have gone

and that the sheep that built this cathedral-like
tall house of god and the portly merchants
    are noticeably unapparent.

The doves are not as holy as they were
as they feed on grain and rape in the widest acres

and from where I sit with my footprint on the brake
of particulates and diesel fumes and Ad Blue

the high ground close to dusk is not the place
to moralise on moon-shots and resources

as Selene climbs above the fields of harvest
and Ceres gazes upwards from a place
    that's blanched and boundless.

The Ash Tree and the Moon

Although transparent
at nearly midnight
my windowpane looks black.

What startles is the moon
a fully rounded red arresting fact
like a corpuscle, a clot, in some dark vein

that's rising like
a cardiac event

a slow attack
on my dull senses.

Anaemia the only risen hope
as this distended redness,
climbs, contracts, like a cell that whitens.

And as I watch this thought, this artefact,
that's in effect imagination's bubble
it tangles in the arteries that track
the vascular commitment of this ash
    when it comes to
        heartwood.

Phishing

I'm trying different baits: bread flake, sweetcorn,
hempseed; anything to tempt a 2lb roach
    from its private space.

I'm willing it (suspended as it is)
in the mill pool's depths of senseless disbelief
to open up a line, some chink of light
where I can start to reach into a mind
that thinks it's closed to falsity

    – persuasion –

to get this canny cyprinid to slip –
to click on a virtual link in the virtual shine
of reflected and refracted things that dazzle
    as the hook bamboozles.

The Inspectorate of Spectres

Ghosts from the past are becoming commonplace:
The edges of my sleep are overcrowded –
my dreams cramped.

Some of the ghosts are still alive
which wouldn't please them if they knew
    – but I'm not telling –

I toss and turn all night in familiar places
that have suddenly turned strange.

The bridleway I walked through as a child
beneath the elms, beside the leaf-full ditches
is full of pilgrims from the past and from the present –
   perhaps the future:

The one-eyed man, the witch,
the sailor without a ship,
the evangelical lady singer,
the octogenarian seamstress
and people I know today
who are not yet ghosts – but will be:

my partner, my brother, even
the postman is getting in on the act.

Fact or fiction? I don't know.

What's worrying is that it's happening when I'm awake –
I even see images of myself in an infinite number
of multi-universal bridleways wending their way
    towards nowhere – endlessly.

It's the smell of fermenting leaves that I find the worst
rotting apples, humus, memories of fog, the first frost –
winter.

Panning the Mind for Rudd

The cuckoo, more like a hawk in flight, than anything else
traverses its own reflection and the lake
like a hobby or a kestrel
might at speed
when after
prey.

I didn't know they called when on the wing
but as it passed above me, grey on grey,
in a sky as calm and silent as the clouds
      it rang its bell.

I know it's not a church, right here, right now,
but the lake is one vast icon so revered
     by this faithful angler

and if you think such holy thoughts unfound
in a world that's made of calculus and matter
then I'm the missing link and that's no Sanctus
that rings and rings and rings as the moment drowns
      in its mirror image.

Glances and Glissando*

There is a dance above the surface of the lake:
a prehistoric aerial quadrille as darters dart
and hover with such
  wings

        as fine and
      filamentous
    as the silks

that are spun
by spiders.

The hawkers hawked when the dinosaurs were kings
  – of the far Jurassic –

and here today still faceted by light
with as many planes and angles to their eyes
as millennia between such different things as the names of eras
  the quickstep quickens

and in the name of sheer balletic grace
the demoiselles in damask take the floor
to shimmer in their sequins and their satins
as time's metallic tempo slows the pace
to a waltz where each glissade between two notes
  is an image drowning.

* *a continuous slide upwards or downwards between two notes.*

Heavy Metal – A Requiem

How often do we fly tip people's bodies –
bury them in earth with all their toxins
that leach out and poison life with heavy metals
    and like pollutants

or burn them that the air is then infused
with pesticides and other harmful vapours
    that choke the planet?

I'm told that only fungi have the tools
to neutralise such gross contamination
    with spores and hyphae

And I for one am happy to espouse
a living shroud of mushrooms when I die
that I may reinvest in what I came from
without the lie that I was Nature's guest
    with green credentials.

Poppies in June *(for Sylvia Plath)*

Poppy – can you speak:
is your bloody mouth a memory of her death?

Are you a clot in the veins of poetry
or a cell like her mental prison –
some corpuscle of hope in the midst
        of hopelessness?

There are so many questions left to answer -
        so many words unsaid.

Are you vibrant like a glass of wine, like claret,
or dead like a pool at dusk when the sun that sets
        is the night's transfusion?

Are you Mars as all that's sylvan in her name
punctuates the darkest wood with stars
        or the light's full stop?

Echium

Echium as a flower name you say is not poetic
but this green and lilac tower where it leans
in our front garden is a bee-loud lyric.

Who needs such Irish islands in a lough or fancy glades
when we have a concrete driveway and this plant
with its honeyed life of pollen and proboscis

and in our own polite suburban way
we know that our green credentials

    – by subscription –

are purer far than the farmers with their sprays
and the same rotated crops as the red-list widens.

There is no NPK in our small acre:
diversity's the thing as we all say when environmental –

             but the food we eat
           and the fuel we use
        pertain to something other
     but we hide such thoughts
as we feed the birds today

and
the tip
tomorrow.

Echium (2)

I am counting bees, bumble bees, solitary bees and honey bees:
they are climbing a green and lavender tower
that is leaning at an angle in the light
because it has grown too tall –
      too heavy.

The flowers as small as they are, are the vocal cords of the bees:
this is a plant that sings and the song is the sound of summer –
    a hymn to the god of heat.

Bring me nectar I hear him say
and the hot and honeyed thermals of the sun
draws them up in swarms of swarthy velveteen
      into clouds of sweetness.

Denouement

                                    If you
                                    can cope
                                    with silence

without the sound of vowels and consonants
telling their long-learnt constructs and their lies
about such things as loss and lost connections
you may just hear between these specious lines
the phonemes made of starlight and the phrases
that built the moon's vibrations and those tides
unconscious of the stages and the steps
that we have climbed through slime and all its phases
up to the dry rhetorical conceits that poets write
to fill their empty pages and their minds
and if this rhyme offends I'll tell you why:
it's your belief in disassociations
and my contentious paradox implied
that language kills alliances with nature –
that pens and swords are blinded by the light
and all there is of truth resides with silence

and the
death of time.

Principles and Possibilities

When August comes, late August,
and along the summer hedgerows where I walk
the diadem or garden orb, you choose,
hangs its silken radials of light
    all blebbed with dew.

I think of the Fates, the Wyrd, and other spinners
who knew the sheer connectedness of webs
that fascinated mystics in their day
the alchemists and scientists
    – and yes today –
it's quantum physics.

The scabious and willowherb's preamble
along the way to toadflax and to autumn
touches at a tangent some would say
the yellowhammer's drawn out threads of song
that also touch the leaves that slowly tarnish
as sunlight speaks of shadows and the swifts
    and light's migration.

And when the frost inscribes the windowpane
with all these weird geometries of ice
and every branch and blanching bifurcation
is like a tree unfurling into leaf
then what's belief or any observation
when the eye receives uncertainty's decree
    by the way of photons?

Lines

Was this a dark bush cricket
sitting beside me by the river
as I fished for chub?

A dark unconscious consciousness on my holdall
that made me think of bait wrapped up in chitin.

Such long antennae and thin triangular legs
to detect my thought and spring into sudden action

    instinctively.

But are these the facts
are wings and stridulation
any different to tongues
when we talk in terms of language?

I'm no linguist as you can tell
but there's something here between me and this cricket
that is not a magic spell or imagination

but the way my rod tip speaks before it quivers –
before the chub, the hook, and recognition

    strikes

like a match in the brain –
like a book on fire.

Minnows

Splinters of light or shards, it's hard to say:
the minnows dart this way and that
beneath the darkening surface of the river
    as dusk approaches.

Each twist and turn evasive, one assumes,
when perch in hungry shoals peruse the depths
   in their packs of purpose:

even the shoals of roach are on alert
for any quick reversal in their luck
that finds a pike close lurking in the reeds
    like a green torpedo.

A sudden spurt of silver fountains up
into the cusp of daylight and the stars –
a living gush that flickers and falls back
into the moon's presentiment, the facts,
    of its dual dimensions.

"Words" *(for Edward Thomas)*

Fixed and free, he said, as in a rhyme
and in a way it's true – a negotiation.
I watch the way the leaves fill in the lines
between the branches. How seemingly astray

each leaf complies with its formal part
in the wordless game we know as spring.
It's like a cage that catches midnight's heart
and the moon's set phases. The robin sings

in darkness yet maintains a certain song –
each lyric note, each verse within its framework.
And as I watch the moon recite, declaim
between each bifurcation and beyond

I hear the stars and planets as they spin –
conform to a law that fixes – then rescinds.

Storm Ellen 18th August 2020

Will Killimer and Tarbert feel the squeeze
of isobars and gradients of weather
when the ferry and the Shannon disagree
on whether County Clare or County Kerry
should be the proper landing place for thoughts
    that are still inclement?

Twice I've landed there in calmer times
to see the place where half of me was made
      if not conceived.

They have felt the squeeze before
   – ask the O'Donnell's –

and when I placed my feet where Ellen stood
in the greenest rain and the grief of a drowning isle
that year when I came for Yeats and the celebrations

I felt for her sons who
        marched down an English
            street on their way to France

            and for Michael's dreams
      and my own grandmother's heart
that was surely broken

as she sat by her pot-black stove in an East End room
stewing her mash of tea leaves and her words
like an Irish brew in the Cork that Michael knew
    or in Ellen's Kerry.

It's not all Black and White

We have a guest at night:

he's not unwelcome
even though his claws
are sharp and bright
beneath the moon
as he digs for worms.

I can see his stripes
in the dim and moonlit shadows
as he wrecks the lawn with his star-struck appetite
while the tawny owl hoots out with its wise approval.

I'd like to call him brock
but I'm badgered by the mob
to be less folkloric - to be more precise.

I don't know his true taxonomy, his Latin tag,
        but then, nor does he.

Suffice that the worms are fat –
that the dark is damp and the dewfall
well, just right, for his excavations.

As for the lawn I think I'll leave it wild
and when that other star inhabits the brink of dawn
        with its golden eye

I'll look for the pinkest titbits
left behind and perhaps – go fishing.

WINTER

Oilseed Rape – A Carol

Already the rape has risen into light some eighteen inches:
December holds its breath as late November
fills the sky with fieldfares and the sight
    of descending rooks.

St Andrew writes the text of ice and Advent
yet even now the toadflax by the hedge
is like the lambent glow of cloistered candles
    that fade and flicker.

The risen sun strikes gold in a cloudless sky
but like the season's wick its flame is low
    like a hope benighted.

Soon the snow will come with children's voices
that flake and fall across the fields of rape
    like the thought of angels

and suddenly the choices that we make
are overall our heartscape and a sky
    that imagines stars.

Something to Wish Upon

And as the sun is westering at dusk
and a gibbous moon is rising in the east
the winter wheat beside the darkening wood
gathers the swathes of mist around my feet
    as I walk the headland.

I think that frost and maybe freezing fog
will greet the midnight black of winter's heart
where often in the hush of leafless trees
a tawny owl will speak without a word
when all is still and silent save the rush
    of a shooting star.

And maybe now when heat is at a loss
and fieldfares fountain out from every hedge
the mist condensing deeper as the sun
reddens as it settles and subsides
will wrap me in its chill December arms
    like a Christmas ghost.

Frost – New Year's Day

Whiter than Chinese white or virgin snow
the frost on New Year's Day furred in its winter coat
like a mountain hare or ptarmigan
glints in the early light like a star-filled sky
    that awaits the sun.

The silence, more silver than white,
lays its misted strata on the fields
    and across the river.

The bird-less air is dense and thick with light
and as I walk the headland into dawn
I can sense the weather's icy morning hand
    that holds me back.

I need no gold reminders of the songs that augur spring:
it's here when growing old that I belong
where ice on every cracked and creaking puddle
pretends itself as ferns or branching fronds
    to my cold eye.

Where the stoat whose dark and dreaded
summer dress was somehow fearful
expresses now the best of barren hopes
    in a coat of ermine.

I am a man enamoured of the frost
when early rooks in black-beleaguered lines
fly from the sun's uprisen thermal plans
into a mind that warms to the lack of heat
    and the stormcock singing.

Lavenham Woods in Winter

The woods are half-obscured by the early fog:
frozen in space and time by this morning's frost
    and the air condensing.

Nothing will shine today
as the temperature drops
and the land lies dormant.

Perhaps a blackbird's voice
can just be heard on the edge of light –
on the edge of something other than the stars
    and the night's deep freeze.

Across the fields and the white of winter wheat
the shifting veils of grey reveal sheet ice in the frozen furrows
and what we see that's hidden from our sight
is depicted by the mind's ingrained beliefs
    like a song's reprise.

There is a gift of gold that lights the east
beyond the myth of magi and the feast that relies on vision
and somewhere deep and dark in this hidden wood
like the blood that's primed the pump of this cold heart

an aconite like something understood
answers the solar silence as it should
    when the sap is rising.

Two of a Kind

The snowflake is alone and so am I –

    unique some say
    like this six sided
    silent serenade
    that sings of ice.

The two of us are once, not even twice,
a certain susurration in the light –
  no more than whispers.

Listen as we float and slowly fade
into the mute unmentionable dusk
where even ice at midnight melts away
    and the moon is silent.

Out of Obscurity

The fog has left its calling card beside the River Stour –
thin silken threads all furred in white
where spiders hang their webs of light
    by midnight's open door.

The stars have fallen into fog that's fading as I speak
where silver trees have been released
across the blanched unburdened grief
    of daylight's written score.

This sheet's as white as any page
    notated by the rooks.

The sunset slant empurpled rays
of some imagined winter's stave
    beside the River Stour

is suddenly a music played ethereal and pure
    as if a bow was slowly drawn
        across the strings of ice and hoar
            and the swans were thus reborn.

Crystal Saints

Like crystal saints the holy snow
came sidling down the stairs of woe
    into a world of light

and I was there with tongue outstretched
to taste the icy Eucharist on earth
    down here below.

Then on my knees despite the freeze
I prayed at winter's altar
and thanked the god
of ice and fog

  – you've guessed –

                       for
          frozen
water.

And when the alb, the vestment, laid
its cerements cold and white
I knew that shrouds were disallowed
    to my awoken sight.

The crystal saints came sidling down
in whispers without words
and as they fell the Book of Kells

with rubrics like the sun
that sets as daylight rings the knell
of what the night begun

could not relate through any verse
a more enlightened living church
    than hexagons foretell.

The air was thick with frozen stars
  – the invisible transformed –

so many drifts, so many gifts
across the fields that light has kissed
    with silence, like a psalm.

Angels – Gaudete Sunday – December 13th 2020

I'm in need of angels, ethereal beings
tinged with white and gold behind the clouds

    – harps optional –

It's cold in here amongst my winter thoughts -
starless and alone, fraught with all the things
that feed the flesh and not the soul.

I need the seed that flourished in the past –
that flowered in my innocent young heart
    when magic happened.

I still believe that guardians exist
with wings and blue-eyed wonder
in the vast and reimagined Christmas light
    that cleaves all darkness.

I still look round to cast a sudden glance across my shoulder
in case by chance I'll catch that holy glimpse of something other –
of things once taught when reason was apart
    and somewhere else.

This is the season now of simple hearts and granted wishes –
I'll close my eyes beneath this berried branch and kiss a prayer
and when my lids are lifted from the dark
    and light's renewal

snow on snow will feather down the airways unremarked
like harbingers or heralds of the spring
    and the lark's blue heaven.

Wintry

Today it is diagonal:
the rain at a freezing angle turns to sleet
and down the sloping air towards the dawn
    come thoughts of snow.

               We're on the cusp
      between the warmth and cold
of this dark winter

and on my skin
    as daylight travels with me
        where I walk along this road

the touch is that of fingers made of ice
    under midnight stars.

What is it I remember or forget
as the first white flakes like whispers or regrets
    come tumbling down?

             I do not know
      and yet I seem to sense
there's something other.

A crow that does not scare me half as much
as these unbidden fingers on my flesh
erupts like a hidden meaning from the hedge
    and flies away.

Sea Reach & Sandbanks

The brents across the far and ebbing tide
inhabit the distant sandbanks and the ooze
and their presence though unseen by the watching eye
is known by the cronk and croak that is their reply
    to the misted silence.

They are more like barking dogs
than feathered guests from the frozen tundra –
these fowl unleashed from ice and its tightening grip
remind us that the light is still defined by the season's limits.

And now again, far out by the cold sea reach,
a clanking buoy and the clanking chains of geese
touch the occluded moment like a sign
    or forgotten symbols.

Between the Trees at Midnight

Along this road that I've always travelled
between the midnight trees and above the dip
    that dawn will deck with frost

a whiteness in the splay of my full beams
hangs its suspended shape in the midnight dark
    that is now enlightened.

Time stops
when such surprises
come to pass as we journey on:

when what was once familiar and true
becomes the dream of difference, something other –
an instant that redeems our sleeping hearts

    – this living nightmare –

and then this ghost, this unexpected star, that hangs
its eternal meaning and its hope in some holy stasis
resumes as a barn owl must when it's less bizarre
    the regime of movement.

Winter Solstice – A Dilemma

What can we solve when faced with contradictions?
The earth revolves around this sphere of gold
    as it spins in space

and we are told that only through its axis
    do we know the seasons.

It's cold out here at dawn and the frost still thickens
but deep within the heart and this earth's crust
    the fire burns.

The morning star at dusk we know as Venus
or Hesperus for the mythically inclined

is now another name that fades and flickers
as Lucifer, the fallen, comes to mind
    on the dim horizon.

Now that I'm old I need no resolutions
as Janus-like I sit on the solar cusp
    and look both ways.

The light and dark may need their revolutions
to find each other's differences explained
but time and I are done with such restraints

for we know that all that quickens and confuses
like aconites held fast in winter's chains

will soon enough be proof, if proof's required,
that ice and fire are in fact the same.

The clouds have drawn a sharp delineation
northwest/southeast across the morning sky –

blood red and blue the choice, the demarcation,
that none can choose when two from one is taken
      and thought defined.

A Moment in the Mist

There is the silence of the sun in river mist
as the morning stuns the meaning of the light
      with hints of gold.

There are seagulls at a tangent to my mind
as down the air they overcome the night
and sidle into flurries, white and rare,
      like flakes of snow.

I know that rooks and jackdaws can't requite
the chaste remembered love that Advent brings
when raucously their black December lives
      are full of contrast.

There is the silence of the sun in river mist
as winter burns the last of summer's embers
and time itself resists those hives that hum
      and the ring doves' anthem.

The Drumbeat of the Stars

I am watching and listening
and what do I see
and hear?

I see the blue and cirrus of a sky that's turning chill
and hear in the fallen aspect of the wind
a music that relates the dying year
through the leaves
that whisper.

There is as the whisper dies a certain stillness
that veers from the warming south into colder climes
     that unnerve the spheres.

What was gold no longer glisters down the air
when the robin's autumn requiem belongs to the frozen light
     of the coming season.

Try as I might to avoid the spider's snare
as the dew point touches silence and each web
    with a prayer that sparkles

I know that at night Orion stalks the moon
as the clouds in silver somnolence despair
    like a dream awoken

and higher still the stars as they paradiddle
with their frosty, vast, abysmal, loud tattoo
rattle the repercussions of my heart
    with their muffled drums.

Snow at Midnight

I remember the moon back then in 87:
how snow eight inches deep
found me walking out along the streets
    towards the Plough

  – an inn not the constellation.

Uncannily the silence and the moon,
framed as it was by the light and dark relief
    of the blazing clouds

     – the cumuli –

I sensed like
a gauge or a pointer
under glass an approaching storm.

The moon, full-rounded, and unreasonable,
hung suspended over the park like a predatory eye

    – amber and alert –

All was frozen into silhouettes:
shadows and a strange glow
like embers in a grate –
glimmering.

There is cold that affects the flesh
and a chill that goes far deeper –
into the very soul, like the stars that shine
    and shimmer – silently.

Prescience or no - I couldn't say
but midnight came with snow like I'd never seen –
     a vertical snowstorm.

As dry as dust and as white as wedding veils
     the storm intensified.

I found myself cocooned in the muted moment
as if life and death existed somewhere else:
two feet or more of even snow
too dry to squeeze
together –

                         the weather's
                  frozen ashes
            ice and isolation
       an absolute
like zero.

A Fox at Dawn

This morning in Barrow Hill I saw a fox:
spotlit as it was as I made my way
between the fields of sugar beet and frost
where my headlights and the hint of a frozen dawn
became as one in the depths of a deepening winter

   – I stopped to wonder.

What is this wonderland we talk about
as we watch this russet renegade from night
searching the ditch and headlands for a bite
      we take for granted?

I parked, turned out the lights and left the car:
I began to walk downhill as the sun came up
and felt what the fox must feel when the hands are numb
      and the features blue.

It was then that my love of frost and snow and ice
      was put to the test:

that all my past expressions of delight
in those words of whiteness
began to thaw.

I saw without my eyes
      what the fox had seen
            in the fragile light

as the crystalline contrivance of the air
took on the sheen of silence where it glittered.

No need to overstate these final lines
enough that the sun begins its daily climb
into the warm remembrance of the spring –

that the puddles and the furrows thick with ice
ring to the great tit's trebles as they chime
      and the dark decreases.

SPRING

Weathering

When the weather's blue and the world is green
and the shadows flow in waves across the wheat
and the distances are dusky with their trees
    and their misted focus

then the lens through which I see is the lens of May
where the buzzard mews in circles overhead
and the first of the white dog roses in the hedge
    (suffused with pink)

are all made
of light –

when the focal length is infused with the year's first haze
and the wheat more blue than green under building clouds
that accumulate and climb to amazing heights
    where they blaze with gold

then the nerve that connects my eyes to my thinking brain
is alive to the swoop and swerve of the swallow's wings
as they link in a way uncertain and absurd
the outer and the inner and such things
    as our human weather.

Two Rooks - Two Species

Two rooks have started to use my feeding station:
a breeding pair I should think –
black with a purple sheen,
an iridescence.

They strut with a rare belief
in their own importance
and I must concur.

The baldness of their beaks has an air of business –
a middle-aged assertiveness

   – such status –

that their place in the pecking order has conferred.
They are welcome guests at my humble human table
         – my food is theirs –

all I ask in return
is access to their otherness –
   communion.

Crime Report

It's in its right place you might think
as its thin proboscis sips at the
sunlight's handiwork:

stigma, stamens, ovary,

enough to keep one busy one would think –
pollen to eat, nectar to drink, heaven.

But no its wings are wayward
    – desultory –

It tries another flower, then another,
and then with bags of gold it lumbers off
as cumbersome as a crime so nearly bungled -
    a repeat offender.

Stall Light

When I worked on the Downs in Wiltshire
marking the fields as the Pawnee* reached the clouds
and turned on its sunlit axis and almost stalled
in the gilt and gilded air as the red light shimmered.

Before the level flight across the sheen
of winter wheat and hares as
the NPK flared like
the spread of
buckshot

in a scene – an uncertain image.
I was aware of Avebury and such things
        – all supposition –

like months and moons and solstices and circles
like buzzard's wings still soaring here and now
as spiral thoughts genetically impinged
on time's unsolved ecliptic as we spin
        and light still shimmers.

The Pawnee climbed again like a name demeaned
a metallic high new totem – an appropriation –

as the red light gleamed and the aircraft almost stalled
and the fall was just a construct and its wings
        a cruciform conventional conceit

                                as I marked the fields
            and the winter wheat grew tall
and the hares grew thinner.

*Piper Pawnee - small single winged aircraft use in crop spraying

Art Lesson

There's a muntjac in the garden
doing what muntjac do to leaves and branches.
But that's okay; it's like having a second gardener –

animated shears, a fur-lined yet silent chainsaw.
She's quite attracted to seeds fallen from the feeders –
peanuts and fat-balls if she can get them.

It's strange to be on safari in a bungalow in Suffolk:
the kitchen window is a work of art, a wildlife painting.
It sometimes frames a badger or a fox, a hungry pheasant.

Right now there's a common buzzard at a height
soaring on the sky's taut canvas and as I watch
with an inartistic eye it draws a circle – freehand.

Waiting for a Bite

Demoiselle or damselfly just names
as they shift their glint metallics round the lake
        on wings of light.

Metallic sheens of blue and vibrant red
        – even yellow –

spread their Maytime message
through the sedge
and over
lilies.

For sex they form a tandem, then a wheel –
a steamy scintillation in the heat
that circulates the mystery of life
and what we feel for love and for each other
    when the spring enlivens.

A singleton, one only can assume,
mistakes my thin red float for a loveless partner
and perches on its tip like a perfect suitor
        on the perfect date.

But then when this bright idea
        – upon reflection –

sinks as the float slips sideways and is gone:
this lone and lovelorn amorous Narcissus
hangs on the flimsy wings of a drowning thought –
        and a heartless echo.

An Exhumation of the Mind

In Barrow Hill I've found no tumulus –
no burial of history's ups and downs
    in a mound of earth.

All I see with this cold eye of calculation
is the yearly round of oilseed and barley –
of sugar beet and winter wheat and a sky
   with its rooks and jackdaws.

   But if I look more closely
     just a little harder

I can see on the corvids' wings a purple sheen
    – an iridescence –

and higher up like a star with the blackest song
a skylark hangs on air like a lyric theme
    that's devoid of time

where history both stops and is reasserted
by so many birds awoken, disinterred
   by the pen's exposure.

August in May

This is August in May:
the thermals and thermometers have risen
beyond the scales of even centigrade
    as the pavements blister.

This is the burn that flared in the Book of Daniel –
the Shadrach, Meshach, moment in the furnace
where they and hot Abednego were saved
    by the grace of God.

I've broken an egg and cooked it here today
    on this flagstone hob
in the way that I remember in the fifties
when summers were always hotter
    – or so they say –

despite the
global climate and
the facts in the yearly data.

This exponential rising of the heat
can also find its chapter in the Bible
but who could ride a horse through such a fire
to meet the last inferno that we meet
    when each act is stifled.

Instead in May with August on its mind
I'll look for the shade that's not the shades
            – chthonic –

I'll lie back beneath this awning thus reclined
in a dreamy, drowsy sweat, like a melting ice cap
        in a sea that's rising.

Ai Ai*

I am a writing machine turning the outside inside
and then into reams of readable paper.
    Readable you say?

    A matter of opinion.

The bluebells are non-scripta in the woods
but I have written out their deep blue meanings.

I am writing because I have to:
the ink is running out but my fingers
and the qwerty act as one and the words keep coming –

    tap, tap, tap,

like a beetle in the rafters of a mind that is now obsessive.
'Save as' is the remedy for time
    in its timeless files.

My memory is a memory stick:
a 64 plus gigabyte device –
a vicarious and virtual
    strange life.

This lexicon of language, its genetics
will survive the coded failings of the flesh
in a binary remembrance of a life when one is zero.

*Ai Ai: Hyacinthoides non-scripta (the bluebell) is a species in the genus Hyacinthus. Non-scriptus means "unlettered" or "unmarked" to distinguish this plant from the hyacinth of Greek mythology. This mythical flower, which wasn't the modern hyacinth, grew from the blood of the dying prince Hyacinthus. His lover, the god Apollo, shed tears that marked the flower's petals with the letters "AIAI" ("alas") as a sign of his grief.

One Thought - Infinite Expressions

Even this house is biblical, made of clay:
the windows are transparently looking back
to glacial sands and memories of glasswort.

The road remembers water and the melt
when ice was turned to shingle and the sea
laid down its white and sedimentary thoughts
    and called it chalk.

The blackbird has a star caught in its throat
    that can't stop singing

and as I walk these warm suburban streets
that are a psalm, a song, a celebration,
the summer heat reminds me who I am
and where I live in nature's rearrangements.

True Love

I'm not really sure what's best:
the fishing or the nightingale
whose rest is always
    woken –

the lily pads, the float, the thought of tench
or this full-throated song without request
  from the sunlit woods.

Or is it yet the campion in red
that rouses springtime passions from a bed
  that's as yet unspoken?

The kite that soars
the cuckoo's ringing bell
the swallows when the door is open wide
to mayflies and the hatch of warming air
that climbs into the blaze of cumuli
    that are blinding white.

Or is it rudd that catch the angler's eye with fevered gold
as they pan the silver seams of bream and roach
deep in the darkest ore of a secret lake:
for a hidden sign –
for a certain
totem.

And when the swallow slakes its Maytime thirst
across the swathes and surfaces of light that gleam and glitter
is it the fish, the flowers, or the fowl,
that touch the angler's heart with unwritten vows –
    like a love requited?

A Concrete Proposal

Being apart for weeks, each of us in isolation,
you by the sea and me further north
        – inland –
      in open country

is not redeemed by our virtual conversations -
WhatsApp and Skype poor substitutes for relationships.

You have the creeks and saltings that I miss
as you walk the dogs to the sound of the last brent geese
    and the plaintive curlews.

For me it's the soaring buzzard in the heat
drawing its magic circles overhead
as it rides the warming thermals on the back
     of a locked-down April.

I miss as well those simple human things that I never thought of:
the gentle touch on the back of a partner's hand –
an affectionate meeting of the lips
for nothing more or less
than the heart's
address

for a need unspoken.

It doesn't matter now that we're growing old –
that our once so fervent schemes in the name of love
have slowed to the less impatient urgent themes
of constancy and care and even friendship.

But the distance of desire never lessens
between the curlew's isolate Amen
and the buzzard's circulatory response
    to the sky's seduction.

What I miss is the proximity, the warmth,
that human blood can issue when the skin
is touched by the lover's hand and the eyes rescind
    what was once abstraction.

Angel

If you could say that light was like the sea
a heavy thing more dense and deep than water
then you could swim to meet the morning lark
that hovers on the zenith of a song
    and drowns in gold.

It would be wrong to not believe in angels
as this small bird held up by gilded wings
denies what you might see, as well, absurd
    in such a heaven.

But I have swam up there

  – not just in dreams –

but in the blue-unfathomed nether sky of my own mind
and on the way, beyond the sun-struck leaves,
above the earth's green patchwork
and the brown and
harrowed
fields:

the themes that time relies on –
I have seen what some would see in terms of vision
the commonplace uncommon light redeemed
    by a song and feathers.

Hedge Sparrow *(for W H Davies)*

I think it belongs to a dunnock
this thin and scratchy song:

polystyrene rubbed on glass perhaps

    – perhaps not –

It's very hot for May - sizzling:
this song also sizzles
like fat in a pan
when frying
bacon.

Hedge sparrow, hedge accentor, hedgibet:
so many names for this bird in bedraggled duds –
    this itinerant whistler.

I too have known
        the underside of hedges
                in the sun – on walkabout

and even now assessing this squeaky trill, this treble,
like chalk across Welsh slate, a blackboard,
I scratch my head when trying to recall
    the eggs – the hedge school.

An Unwritten Stanza

The self-heal is in bloom
and because of its name
and its curative possibilities
I pick a single flower.

There is a room in the self –
a stanza that's as yet unwritten.

A space that's always there
   like a bud in winter:
      each petal furled
against the thought of spring –

the idea
of light.

These hints can be resisted
in their season –
when reason dies
and the written verse
      is silent.

I look to the violet petals
   – the corolla –
and the purple calyx
and see no healing essence
just the self and its scent –

      divided.

The lawn is in its violet covered shrouds
and purple drapes like Lenten statues

obscuring the sculpted
symbols of the saints
the immaculate Virgin

– the Logos.

The season in my hand
is all but nameless
as the petals start to open –
show their face.

The unwritten stanza
attracts the sun's proboscis
and a bee:

the ink runs dry –
the language
sweetens.

Starstruck without Theories without Strings

There's no such thing as nature:
there is just what there is inside and out
so why should we externalise a thought
when thoughts confuse and leave us only doubts
    and names to play with?

There are no things without but not within –
no clouds except where water disallows
ideas of fog and frost and snow and rain
when all it seems is hidden in the shrouds
      of unseen vapour.

Do not explain the mystery of sound
when silences astound us without words
and starlight like a song that's sung aloud
in every throat of every singing bird
is but a chord, a deep vibrating thread,
that something weaves like silken-ness within
when nature is no longer seen without
and the spider plucks the heart's internal strings
    and the stars are centred.

The Borderlands of Light

It is autumn in the borderlands of spring:
the singing birds have stopped
and St Valentine has lost the golden ring
    of the light's betrothal.

The marriage of the seasons and the sun
        has been annulled –

obscurity divides these two dark souls
where frost has whitened something like resolve
only to be disheartened by the fog
that draws its veils of greyness, like a vow,
        without a wedding.

The only hope conceived of opens flowers –
the yellow and the white of love's bouquet
where aconites and snowdrops spread their shrouds
as if to say that death has passed us by

        – has gone away.

And then a bee and daffodils aloud
proclaim in the velvet hush with a vernal sound
that the sun is a transubstantial living host
as it sails through the silver monstrance of a cloud
    with the song thrush singing.

Fingerposts - February

It is sunny and warm and windy
and a chaffinch in the sunstruck winter branches
trills before it rattles into sparks –
    into spring's ignition.

The river's dash and dazzle into swathes
as gusts increase or lessen, like remarks
    on lambs and lions

is secretive enough amongst the whispers
phragmites makes in lulls that never last
    but say so much.

Is that the summer's voice I hear far off –
the clear and rounded syllables of light
that doves deliver warmly from the heights
    of oaks and alders?

And are the demoiselles a sheer delight
in red and blue and green
unseen metallics

as a spatterdock upholds its yellow cup
quite unbelieved, suspended in my mind,
as a chaffinch trills and rattles in the park
    and a brimstone startles?